For **Lucas** and **Ariella** who inspire me every day with their big feelings and wonderful imaginations.

Hard at work identifying all the emotions reflected by each animal on the first page!

My Mama Says

Inside me lives a Village

Written by Nadine Levitt
Illustrations by Miriam Mitzi Rosas

Printed in Canada
First Printing, 2019
ISBN 978-0-578-53566-1
www.MyMamaSays.com

My mama says that inside me
lives a village.

Sometimes she sees a GROUCHY snapper,
who got up on the wrong side of bed.

He's as mean as a hungry tiger

and hot-tempered
like a bear.

Sometimes she sees a SAD sullen pup,
who's down in the dumps and blue.

He's stuck in a cloud with a heavy heart
and tears that blur his view.

Sometimes she sees a HAPPY grasshopper
bouncing around with a smile.

Excitedly he sings and dances
- happy all the while.

Sometimes she sees the **ANGRY** hippo,

who stomps his feet
with a huff AND a puff.

He's mad and he listens to no one,
and he REALLY wants to play rough!

Sometimes she sees the GOOFY goat,
who loves to entertain!

With a silly billy grin, he pretends
to be a crane.

Sometimes she sees the **SHY** little mouse,
who's afraid of the unknown.

He likes to hide between her legs and
he's slow to say hello.

Sometimes she sees the **CUDDLE** muffin cat,
who won't get off her lap.

He snuggles in close

and holds on tight,
like he's ribbon to her gift wrap.

She says there are many more to meet in
the village that lives inside of me.
I should get to know them and say hello
when they visit, even fleetingly.

17

They're made of big feelings I have in me,
so they're more than just make-believe.

But I can tell them what to do
- I can even ask them to leave.

And I should never be afraid
of the dark or the unknown...

For with a village inside of me,
I am never alone.